KLIMT & FASHION

© Assouline Publishing
601 West 26th Street, 18th floor
New York, NY 10001
USA
Tél.: 212 989-6810   Fax: 212 647-0005
www.assouline.com

ISBN : 2-84323-417-4
Translated from French by Uniontrad

Color separation : GEGM (France)
Printing by Grafiche Milani (Italy)

KLIMT & FASHION

CHRISTIAN BRANDSTÄTTER

ASSOULINE

"Women's fashion! A horrible chapter of cultural history, telling us about the hidden desires of humanity...". The fundamental article that Adolf Loos wrote in 1898 ("Damenmode", in *Ins Leere Gesprochen 1897-1900*, Innsbruck, Brenner Verlag, 1932) and contributed to the debate on the reform of women's fashion, started in this passionate tone. This general debate set the European continent ablaze at the dawn of our century after simmering in America and England from the 1850s. Always beautifully dressed in the English style, this elegant architect also owed some of his biggest Viennese commissions to men's tailors, such as the famous house on Michaelerplatz for the clothing firm Goldman & Salatsch, or the Knize and Leschka shops in the Graben. According to him, women, who were immersed in the war of the sexes and fighting for equal rights, were still dependent on the complicated and artificial masculine sensuality: wearing dresses that stood out by their ornamentation and colors, "creating effects with velvet and silk, flowers and ribbons, feathers and colors," they hoped to crystallize the love of men, and, at the same time, win their own emancipation. And when women's legs were timidly starting to bare themselves, freed from these long skirts that covered them up – but consequently devoid of any charm in the eyes of men – it was not due to any great social change, but rather due to the fact that women had conquered certain sports, cycling in particular.

however, everyone had something to say in this debate on clothing "reform": doctors and health advocates were concerned about freeing women's waists; as for suffragettes and advocates of women's rights, they were concerned about freeing their spirits, while everyone else wanted to remove their lace corsets from them: and German nationalists were already sounding the bugle against the diktat of Paris fashion and issuing a call to arms against the decadent rustling of ruched skirts. By a love of aesthetics, many artists joined this movement in order to save this new freedom that seemed condemned to the more comprehensive austerity of dress.

In the beginning, clothing reform was only one aspect among many of these emancipation movements that aimed to change life. It had even become monotonous: the ideological craze did not leave any room for other ornamentation; a blue stocking lay dormant under each uniform gown. Mistreated, even deformed, until now for aesthetic and erotic purposes, the female body was now going to be dressed according to the criteria of hygiene and function only. "Anti-fashion dresses" or "personal dresses" began to be talked about, then very quickly "sacks of potatoes" or "reform sacks," which clearly meant that the women themselves were not ready yet to emancipate themselves from the labels of the fashion makers. While it only took account of the functional aspect of the dress – losing the aesthetic aspect of fashion on the way – the clothing reform could never rival real "Parisian or Viennese chic."

It is at this time that the Secession artists came onto the scene at the turn of the century. While they were against the tradition of revolutionary ideas like the ideas of those who wanted to change life, they cherished above all the dream of a "total work of art," into which fashion should be integrated. Thus, in his work *Das Künstlerische Kleid der Frau* [Woman's Artistic Dress], the German painter Alfred Mohrbutter sowed dreams of emancipation in the hearts of German women; whilst the architects Peter Behrens, Bernhard Pankok and Richard Ricmerschmid exhibited their own sketches at fashion exhibitions; and Henry van de Velde, the multi-talented Belgian artist, decreed the following in his manifesto work *Die Künstlerische Hebung der Frauentracht* [Artistic Improvement of Women's Dress]: "From now on, fashion exhibitions fall into the category of art exhibitions."

I n 19th century Vienna, considered to be the fashion Mecca after Paris, the creativity of such artists allowed the "anti-fashion dress" to set itself up against the frippery of the clothing of the time, but it did not manage to establish itself in the long term. The reason for this failure was twofold: on the one hand, Spartan aestheticism was never established in this "metropolis that had an imaginative and chic taste in clothes"; on the other hand, it was extremely tempting for the Secession artists themselves to put their maxims to the test, they who wanted art to invade all areas of life – but not in the mixed up form that women's clothing was offering. In a typically Viennese way, they "worked around it": they did not abandon the objectives of simplicity and functionality, they made them fashionable, they transformed them into something decorative, wearable, by stripping them of their boring ideals. Many designers took this route. For example, Alfred Roller, an early Secession artist who was the genial companion of Gustav Mahler – had collaborated in his new productions at the Vienna Opera – creating housecoats inspired by Slavonic costume for Mileva, his Croat wife. Koloman Moser, co-founder of the Wiener Werkstätte (Viennese Workshop), designed "reform" dresses for his wife, Dita, and the other members of his family, in an austere black and white style: this 'square style' (*Quadratl-Stil*) would also mark his artwork with the Wiener Werkstätte.

the Wiener Werkstätte's fashion department, the branch that was to experience the greatest commercial success later, formed a separate chapter that only opened from 1911. This department was more interested in fashion than arguing for reform. Following the example of Paul Poiret – the great reformer of Paris fashion and friend of Viennese culture – it was going to oust all of the "thigh-girdles," corsets and "culs de Paris" that had been set up against the reform movement, by offering more appealing methods. It resuscitated the Empire dress, created fabrics with multi-colored patterns and full of imagination, and thus gave birth to a new type of woman.

Viennese artists took part in the debate on reform only by delivering a few sketches: thus, they kept to themselves, almost as a family, influencing as best they could a small circle of the middle class, already clients of their works of art. In this artistic milieu, Gustav Klimt, figurehead of the Secession and the circle that formed naturally around him – a group that would leave the Secession in 1905 – remains an exception. He was the only one to succeed, for a brief moment, in reuniting art, reform and fashion in a harmonious trinity.

W as Klimt predestined to become interested in fashion in such a unique and personal way? He was certainly a partisan of the reform movement, consisting essentially of intellectuals and artists rallied around its criticism of the modern mass society that was hatching at the time. Most importantly, he had chosen Emilie Flöge for his mistress and she was at the head of one of the most prominent couture houses in Vienna.
While it is hardly surprising that Klimt sympathized with the reformers, his favorite clothing – an indigo blue smock – exists as evidence: not only did he love to wear this smock that came down to his feet during the fresh summers he spent on the banks of lake Attersee, but he also wore it when working in his Vienna workshop or outside. This "Klimt smock" – which resembled the oriental caftan and Japanese costume – certainly symbolized for him the return to the simple and natural life to which he partly aspired. In Klimt's character, the robust countryman will always be at odds with the sophisticated city-dweller. Full of sporting ambitions, the artist fenced and wrestled with his male models. His friends smilingly nicknamed him "the athlete"…
In Vienna, he started his days by exercising with dumbbells, then he would take a 45-minute walk to Schönbrunn – a ritual that would continue throughout his life. This body overflowing with vitality was

obviously at its happiest during the two months of summer. Walks, boat trips and swimming, fresh air and the surrounding countryside acted like a fountain of youth for Klimt. The gap that existed, at least from the outside, between his life and his work had already shocked his contemporaries: after they first met in 1907, Egon Schiele – visibly surprised – described Klimt as a "strapping, austere and suntanned" man. But it was Hans Tietze, art historian, who best described Klimt's hybrid character, which not only concerned his physical appearance but finally invaded his whole personality: "a revolutionary of the old school, a sophisticated primitive, a mix of sex-maniac and ascetic, man of the world and monk; a generous egoist, given over to his powerful instincts and the most extreme sophistication" ("Gustav Klimts Persönlichkeit. Nach Mitteilungen seiner Freunder", in *Die Bildenden Künste*, Vienna 1919).

From where did this intense sporting ardor and inexhaustible thirst for fresh air and sunlight come? Even though he shared the reform movement's attachment to the idea of a return to nature, in his youth Klimt had – according to the most recent sources – contracted the "love sickness" that had formerly been very widespread: syphilis. Any number of psychological implications can be drawn from this sickness and his fixation on the maternal figure. By these factors, Klimt's image of woman was "divided" into "great ladies" that cannot be approached and "sweet little Viennese women" who are the object of desire. This information sheds some light on a question asked by many Klimt biographers: Gustav Klimt and Emilie Flöge would not have been lovers in the current sense of the term, their relationship probably remained platonic.

However, we can still consider Emilie Flöge to have been Gustav Klimt's mistress: the artist felt deeply bound to the woman who was to remain by his side from the beginning of the 1890s until his own death in 1918, a feeling that he could not have hoped to find with his friends or fleeting loves. From 1900, he spent nearly every summer with her and her family on the banks of lake Attersee. In Vienna, in everyone's eyes, Emilie Flöge was the woman who shared his life, the woman who accompanied him to all cultural or society events; she gave him serenity and stability, and offered him an unfailing friendship. From 1904, she managed the elegant Flöge Sisters' Salon, which was dedicated to haute couture, with her sisters Pauline and Helene. Klimt encouraged her to turn to the Wiener Werkstätte for the decoration of this studio.

Founded a year earlier, in 1903, by Klimt's friends Josef Hoffmann, Koloman Moser and Fritz Waerndorfer, the Wiener Werkstätte was, so to speak, an extension of the artistic creation of the "Klimt circle" and the Secession. It chose to enclose the caprices of luxury and Emilie Flöge's fashion in a radically functional, strictly geometric studio, decorated in pure tones of black, white and gray. This presentation of "constructive art nouveau" of the Viennese school, was to be rightly celebrated, but was unfortunately broken up and ultimately destroyed in 1938.

Emilie was a smart, sensible businesswoman who had an acute sense of the times. She went to Paris and London twice a year to attend the major fashion shows. She bought the most recent designs there, brought back fabrics and found ideas of designs that she transformed for her own collections, adjusting them to the more generous proportions of the average Viennese woman. Emilie's clientele resembled the clientele that gravitated around Gustav Klimt – generally members of the industrial and financial middle classes – although the designs imported from Paris were also appreciated by ladies of the aristocracy. Liberal and open to new ideas, the customers had a house built by Josef Hoffmann, commissioned the Wiener Werkstätte to do the interior design, asked Gustav Klimt to paint madam's picture and Emilie Flöge to design a dress for her.

As for Klimt, he took care of the brand image of the three sisters' studio. The company logo appeared not only on the letterhead and bills but it was also transformed into a woven label and sewn into each dress. Clearly, the artist did not mind making a little detour through the fields of applied art: in accordance with the reform ideas that were current at the turn of the century, he must even have delighted in playing at dress designer, for Emilie but also with her. It is in this way that Klimt organized a photo session that can be described as exceptional in more ways than one.

It was probably during the summer of 1906 that Emilie Flöge transformed herself into a model for her own studio. With, as a setting, the surrounding countryside, the gently sloping banks of lake Attersee, and the garden of the summer retreat where she and Klimt had taken up residence in Salzkammergut, in Upper Austria, she presented ten variations of 'hanging dresses'. Prototypes of dresses born of the Viennese reform movement, they were created by the hand of an artist but nonetheless conformed to fashion trends.

For this memorable posing session, it was Klimt who was behind the camera, choosing how to center the photo just as he composed his paintings. His objective? To create a catalogue intended for the studio's customers and to give himself a bit of publicity, because the photos were going to be published in the specialized press. It is probable that Klimt thus invented the job of fashion photographer, but it is undeniable that he was the first to take photographs out of doors, and not in the fashion studio, with the avowed intention of publishing them. Studio photography had made its debut in 1901 and baron Adolphe de Meyer, often considered as the first fashion photographer, only started to work for *Vogue* and *Vanity Fair* from 1914.

Emilie Flöge was probably the first model in the world, as suggested by the photographs that Madame d'Ora took of her from 1909. We see her posing in the middle of her studio in artists' dresses created by those who frequented the "Klimt circle". Although, in the association with Emilie Flöge, it is impossible to exactly determine Gustav Klimt's part in the design of the dresses created by the three sisters' studio, the name of the painter clearly appears as the person who took the photographs that were published in January 1907 in the *Deutsche Kunst und Dekoration* – the most important German-language review in the field of decorative arts.

to deduce from this that Gustav Klimt was a fashion designer would certainly be an exaggeration. Because the most beautiful dresses designed by this artist were only ever to be worn by women on canvas and never in reality were these ideal creations derived from a great imagination and applied to fabrics and ornament. Klimt, in his own words, was above all interested in "other people and especially women"; for him eroticism and the rest of the world was found in the "female form". We quote Hans Tietze once again: "The portraits of women that Gustav Klimt painted give the best understanding of the routes he took. Klimt had a deep understanding of what woman is, and, as a real sensual being, created her from within himself; he felt each line of her body and her dresses, each smile and each gesture, seized and flattered each expression of her vitality, but what he paints and draws is not a reproduction of naked reality; his type of woman is both past experience and nostalgia, real and false, an artist's profession of faith. His erotic being, his abandonment to fabrics and at the same time, his mastery, make Klimt a herald of feminine beauty."

With the exception of the patterns he borrowed directly from the fabrics created by the Wiener Werkstätte – for the portraits of *Friederike Maria Beer* (p. 61) and *Johanna Staude* (p. 67) – Klimt always drew on his pure imagination for the various metamorphoses to which he submits the female image in his work. As Ludwig Hevesi – the greatest Viennese art critic of the turn of the century – noted: "[The women] wear dresses made out of the fabrics of today and in accordance with the fashion of today, or almost. This depends on what this 'today' consists of for Klimt. With this amiable penchant for the never that Schiller considered to be the unique eternal [...], this exquisite pinch of improbability that is part of Klimt's romanticism. This unique producer offers us this unique dream setting, these magical combinations that are a delight to the eye. Compositions of elements that the eye had never seen until now and that no one imagined could be combined. This is his imagination. Look deeply into the precious stones that are not, into the splendor and glistening, the multiple gleams of light that cannot be grasped. For the eyes, it's a pure and disembodied joy, the magical recapture of the soul that lived in the art of the body of the splendorous days of old" (*Acht Jahre Secession. Kritik, Polemik, Chronik*, Vienna, Konegan, 1906).

In Klimt's *The Kiss* (p. 36), the most famous icon of Jugendstil [art nouveau], the woman's dress is representative of a dream: the dream of a possible return to paradise thanks to the feminine. Between the glistening gold, the precious decorations and ornaments in the form of a star, the creator Klimt has applied to the fabric of the dress these multi-colored, oval or square fragments consisting of flower gardens, giving us a glimpse of the Garden of Eden, as if through a kaleidoscope.

Bibliography

BRANDSTÄTTER, Christian, "Schöne jüdische Jour-Damen. Gustav Klimts Damenportraits und seine Auftragbeger. Ein verdrängtes Kapitel österreichischer Sammlergeschiche", *in* Stooss, Toni et Doswald, Christoph (Hg.), *Gustav Klimt*, Hatje, Stuttgart, 1992. BRANDSTÄTTER, Christian, *Gustav Klimt et les femmes*, Flammarion, Paris, 1993. DOBAI, Johannes, "Zu Gustav Klimts Gemälde Der Kuß", *in Mitteilungen der Österreichischer Galerie*, thelfth years, n° 56, Österreichische Galerie, Vienna, 1968. KOECK, Hanel, "Mode und Gesellschaft um 1900. Zur Modeszene in Wien", *in* Marchetti, Maria (Hg.), *Wien um 1900. Kunst und Kultur*, Christian Brandstätter Verlag, Vienna, 1985. NEBEHAY, Christian M., *Klimt*, Flammarion, Paris, 1993. STEINER, Ulrike, "Die Frau im modernen Kleid. Emilie Flöge und die Lebensreform-Bewegung", *in* Bayerische Vereinsbank (Hg.), *Gegenwelten. Gustav Klimt - Künstlerleben im Fin de siècle*, Bayerische Vereinsbank, Munich, 1996. VÖLKER, Angela, *Textiles de la Wiener Werkstätte*, Flammarion, Paris, 1994. VÖLKER, Angela, "Kleiderkunst und Reformmode im Wien der Jahrhundertwende", *in* Pfabigan, Alfred (Hg), *Ornement und Askese im Zeitgeist des Wien des Jahrhundertwende*, Christian Brandstätter Verlag, Vienna, 1985.

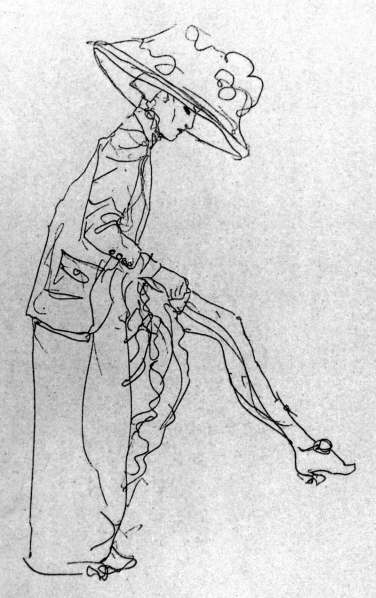

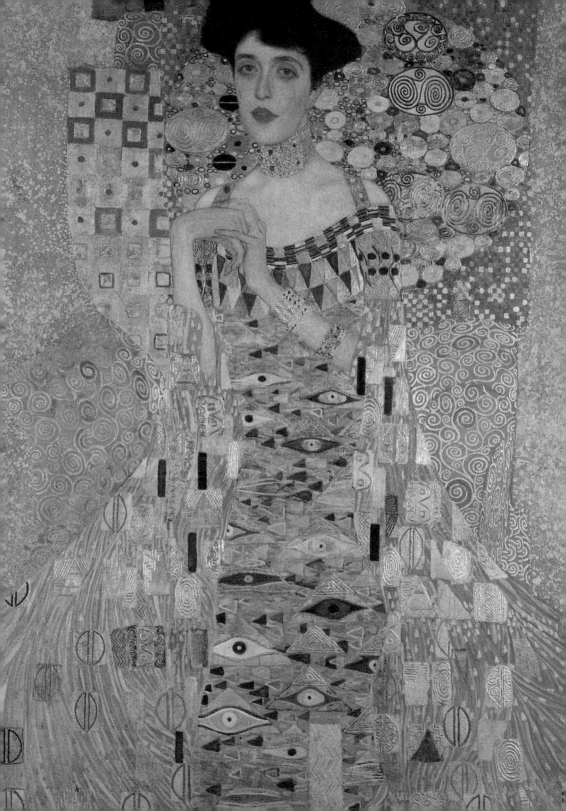

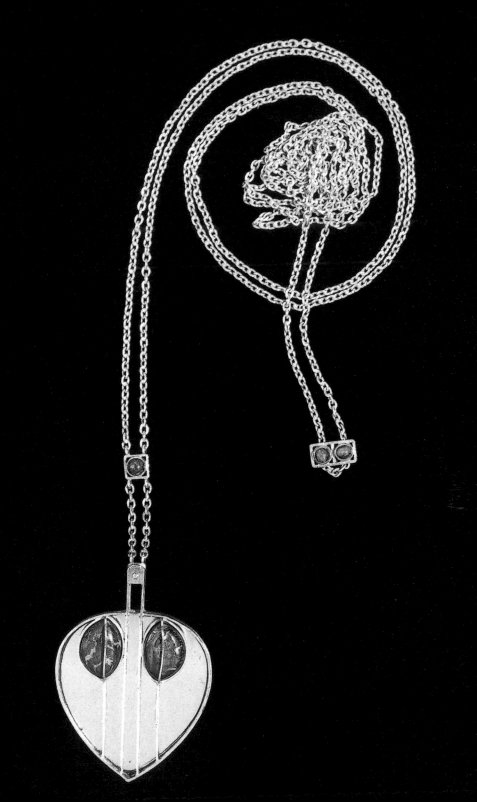

SLOVAKEN STICKEREI

Professor Gustav Klimt
»Konzert-Kleid«.

MARÍA LLIMES

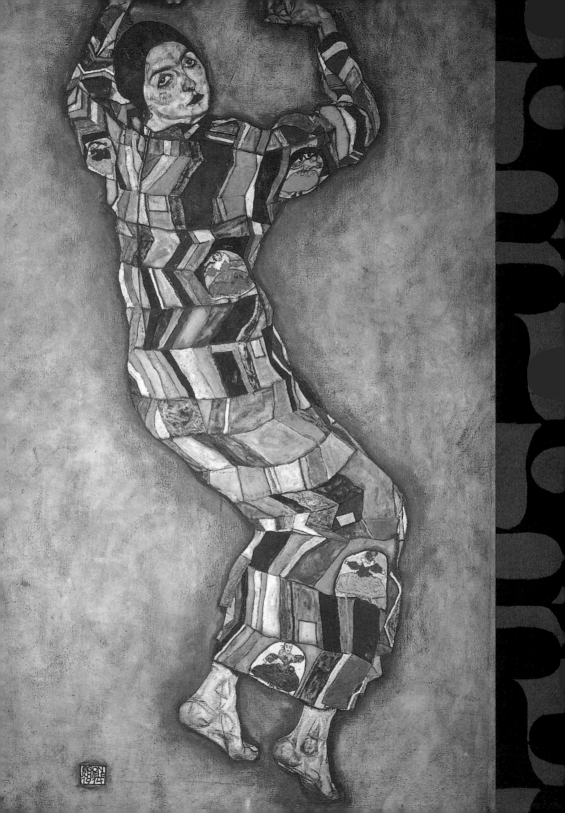

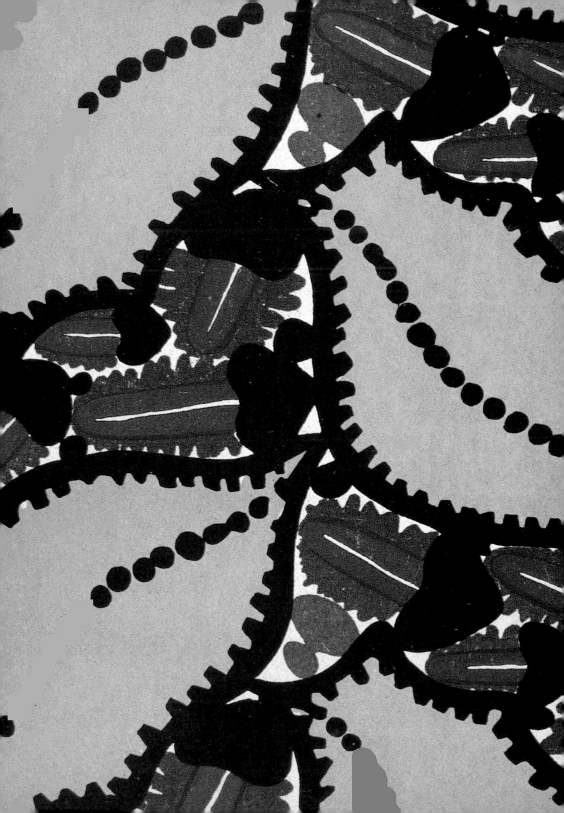

Chronology

1862: Gustav Klimt is born on July 14th in Baumgarten, a suburb of Vienna (currently the 14th district). He is the eldest son of Ernst Klimt (1834-1892) gold engraver, and Anne, nee Finster (1836-1915).

1874: Emilie Flöge, born on August30th. She is the fourth child of Hermann Flöge (1837-1897), manufacturer of meerschaum pipes, and Barbara, nee Stagl (1840-1927).

1876: Gustav Klimt is admitted to the recently opened School of Applied Arts of the Austrian Museum of Art and Industry.

1880: He receives his first commission: the architects Fellner and Helmer commission him to paint the frescos on the ceiling of the Kurhaus (thermal baths) in Karlsbad (currently Karlovy-Vary).

1881: He founds a decorating studio, the Künstlercompagnie [Company of Artists] with his brother Ernst Klimt (1864-1892) and his co-disciple Franz Matsch (1861-1942).

1888: The Künstlercompagnie carries out its first major commission: the decoration of the ceiling and lunettes of the grand staircase of the recently built Burgtheater, for which Klimt is awarded the Croix d'or prize for artistic merit by Emperor Francois-Joseph. Then it is commissioned in 1890 to paint the quoins and piers of the grand staircase of the Vienna Kunsthistorisches Museum.

1891: Membership of the Vienna association of plastic arts artists, called the Künstlerhaus (House of Artists). Helene Flöge (1871-1936), Emilie's sister, marries Ernst Klimt, Gustav's brother.

1892: : Gustav Klimt, Ernst Klimt and Franz Matsch take a studio together at 21 Josefstädter Straße (Vienna VIII).
Death of Gustav's father, then of his brother Ernst (December 9th). The studio that Gustav Klimt shares with Franz Matsch starts to break up.

1897: Klimt and some twenty other artists leave the Kunstlerhaus. Foundation of the Vienna Secession by Joseph Maria Olbrich, Josef Hoffmann and Klimt, who becomes the first president.

1898: *Wer Sacrum* (Sacred Spring), the association's new magazine, is published for the first time (it will be published for six years).
Construction of the Secession building by Joseph Maria Olbrich.
From March to June the first Secession exhibition takes place in premises leased by the Vienna gardening society. Klimt does the poster.

Judith II, 1909, Oil on canvas, 178 x 46 cm.
Galleria d'Arte Moderna, Venice.

1900 : As part of the seventh Secession exhibition, Klimt presents *Philosophy*, the first of three "faculty paintings" intended for the university of Vienna, and the *Portrait of Sonja Knips*.
First summer trip to lake Attersee, where Klimt will return for many summers in the company of the Flöge family and will paint the majority of his landscapes.
Participation in the Paris Universal Exhibition.

1902: For its fourteenth exhibition, the Secession reserves a triumphal welcome for the Beethoven sculpture created by Max Klinger. Klimt paints the *Beethoven Frieze*.
Portrait of Emilie Flöge.

1903: Josef Hoffmann, Koloman Moser and Fritz Waerndorfer found the Wiener Werkstätte (Viennese workshop).
In November-December the eighteenth Secession exhibition takes place (Klimt collection), where eighty Klimt paintings are exhibited.

1904: Josef Hoffmann is commissioned to build the Palais Stoclet in Brussels. Klimt receives a commission for a mosaic frieze in rich materials for the dining room. The Schwestern Flöge (Flöge Sisters) fashion studio opens its doors in Vienna VI, at 1b Mariahilfestraße.

1905: Following tensions, the 'Klimt circle' leaves the Secession.

1906: Klimt designs ten artistic "reform" dresses with Emilie Flöge and for her, in which he photographs her at Attersee.

1907: *Portrait of Adele Bloch-Bauer I.*
The Kiss.

1908: The 'Klimt circle' organizes the 1908 Kunstschau Wien in buildings improvised by Josef Hoffmann on the site where the Wiener Konzerthaus will subsequently be built. The 1909 International Art Exhibition takes place the following year.

1910: Participation in the ninth Venice biennial event.

1911: He participates in the 1911 International Art Exhibition in Rome with eight paintings, winning the first prize for *Death and life*.
The Wiener Werkstätte opens a department dedicated to fashion.

1912: *Portrait of Adele Bloch-Bauer II.*

1917: Klimt is appointed as honorary member of the Vienna and Munich Academy of beaux-arts.

1918: On January 11th, Gustav Klimt suffers an apoplectic attack, followed by partial paralysis. He dies on 6th February 1918 in Vienna General Hospital, leaving many paintings unfinished. His funeral took place on 9th February at the Hietzing cemetery. In the same year, Otto Wagner, Koloman Moser, Egon Schiele..., the Viennese artistic elite of the end of this century, also die.

Lady with fan, 1917-1918
Oil on canvas, 100 x 100 cm

Klimt & Fashion

Portrait of Sonja Knips, 1898. Oil on canvas, 145 x 145 cm. Österreichische Galerie, Vienna. Sonja Knips, whose portrait is considered as the artist's first major portrait of a woman, was a follower of Viennese modernity: in 1903, she commissioned Josef Hoffmann to convert her apartment in Vienna and a villa in the "Wiener Cottage". We see her portrait (left) hung in a room decorated by Josef Hoffman.

Portrait of Fritza Riedler, 1906, Oil on canvas, 153 x 133 cm. Österreichische Galerie, Vienna. In his portraits, Klimt sets up an eternal monument to the new modern woman. He represented this distinguished middle class woman of the turn of the century in all aspects, aware of herself and confident, refined or decadent.

Winter hat, created in 1910 by the Viennese painter Kriser, and photographed by Madame d'Ora (Dora Kallmus), who had the most chic photography studio in Vienna – the d'Ora Studio – where she took society, fashion and theatre photos. **Emilie Flöge in a "summer dress".** Photo taken by Klimt on the banks of lake Attersee during summer 1906, belonging to a series of ten variations of "hanging dresses" created by the painter and his mistress.

Woman putting on her stocking, dressed in an ensemble and wearing a hat, 1910. Pencil drawing, 56 x 36.8 cm. *Woman with hat and feather boa,* 1909. Oil on canvas, 69 x 55 cm. Österreichische Galerie, Vienna. This portrait is not characteristic of Klimt's ornamentation of women, but the face is enhanced with ornaments (hat, boa), which surround her like a halo, a crown.

Gustav Klimt with members of the Vienna Secession, in the main room of the fourteenth exhibition organized around Max Klinger's Beethoven sculpture, for which A. Roller did the poster. From left to right: A. Stark, G. Klimt (sitting on a chair by F. Andri), K. Moser (in front of Klimt, wearing a hat), M. Lenz (lying down). Standing: A. Bohm, W. Lisi, M. Kurzweil (with a hat), I. Stolba, R. Bacher. Seated: E. Stohr, E. Orlik, C. Moll. Photo: Moriz Nahr, 1902.

Portrait of Emilie Flöge, 1902. Oil on canvas, 181 x 84 cm. Historisches Museum, Vienna. Behind the richly ornamented surface, we recognize the fundamental line of the 'reform' dress, which hangs from the shoulders like a sack, and which women wore without a corset. **Emilie Flöge in the Flöge Sisters fashion studio,** leaning on the back of a chair created by Koloman Moser. Photo: d'Ora studio, Autumn 1910.

Study for the portrait of Adele Bloch-Bauer I, 1903. Black chalk, 45 x 32 cm.
Portrait of Adele Bloch-Bauer I, 1907, Oil on canvas, 138 x 138 cm. Österreichische Galerie, Vienna. The portrait of the wife of the great Jewish manufacturer Ferdinand Bloch is considered as the main work of Klimt's "golden" period.

Emilie Flöge, wearing WienerWerkstätte jewelry and a dress that she probably created in collaboration with Klimt and that she wore on the opening day of the "Kunstchau Wien 1908". Photo: d'Ora studio, 1908-1909. **Emilie Flöge,** in the garden of Klimt's studio (Vienna VIII, Josefstadter Straße). She is wearing a "reform" dress, probably designed by Koloman Moser. Photo: Moriz Nahr, 1905-1906.

Heart-shaped pendant necklace, circa 1905. Silver, mirror and two opals. This piece of jewelry, designed by Josef Hoffmann and made by the Wiener Werkstätte, was given to Emilie Flöge by Klimt. **Emilie Flöge,** in the Flöge Sisters' fashion studio. She is wearing a dress that is visibly influenced by Paul Poiret: narrow Empire line, drawn in under the chest, neck edged with a band of fabric, delicate embroidery with flower sepals in the center of the dress. Photo: d'Ora studio, Autumn 1910.

Emilie Flöge in "summer dress." Two photographs belonging to the series taken by Klimt at Attersee during the summer of 1906. An important fashion figure in Paris and Vienna, Emilie Flöge lived in two worlds, reflected by her clothes: the avant-garde world of Klimt, which will give birth to these perfectly unique artist's dresses (photographed here), and the world of the Flöge studio, where the experimental aspect was erased to satisfy customers devoted to the latest Parisian designs.

Emilie Flöge in the Flöge Sisters' studio. Photo: d'Ora studio, Autumn 1910. *The Kiss,* 1907-1908. Oil on canvas, 180 x 180 cm. Österreichische Galerie, Vienna. These two lovers intertwined and haloed with gold is certainly the most famous icon of art nouveau. The differentiation of the ornamental motifs of the two sets of clothes — "hard" rectangular shapes for the man and "soft" sinuous shapes for the woman — make the contrast between power and delicacy.

Fitting rooms of the Flöge Sisters' fashion boutique, fitted out by Josef Hoffmann and Koloman Moser, work carried out by the Wiener Werkstätte, 1904.
Portrait of Adele Bloch-Bauer II, 1912. Oil on canvas, 190 x 120 cm. Österreichische Galerie, Vienna. This portrait is considered as the first remarkable example of the very colorful style that will mark Klimt's final paintings.

Three dresses with Slovak embroidery, Eduard Josef Wimmer-Wisgrill. Pencil on graph paper, circa 1910. Wimmer-Wisgrill managed the fashion department of the Wiener Werkstätte. His designs demonstrated a permanent dialogue with Paris fashion in general and Poiret's fashion in particular.
Mileva Roller, wife of the painter Alfred Roller, is wearing a "reform" dress, inspired by traditional Slavonic costumes. Photo: d'Ora studio, circa 1910.

Tunic made out of "Apollo" fabric, designed by Josef Hoffmann. Anonymous photograph, published in the Wiener Werkstätte "Fashion" photographic album, 1911. **"Apollo" fabric,** Wiener Werkstätte, designed by Josef Hoffmann. Sample, 1910-1911. It should be noted that Hoffmann decided to create a fashion unit within the Wiener Werkstätte when he noticed that a customer's clothes can spoil the harmony of the interior architecture.

Emilie Flöge wearing the "Concert" dress, with a pendant by Josef Hoffmann (see p. 32). Photo belonging to the series of ten variations that Klimt made, during the summer of 1906 at Attersee, of the "hanging dresses" created by Emilie Flöge and himself. **Emilie Flöge** in an artist's "reform" dress at Attersee. Anonymous photo, circa 1910. In order to do away with corsets, dresses flare into a full shape, like smocks, allowing complete freedom of movement.

Klimt and the Flöge family on a boat. From 1900, Gustav Klimt will spend nearly every summer with Emilie Flöge and her family on the banks of lake Attersee, where he will create many of his landscapes. The two companions had chosen to live in the garden of the summer retreat in Salzkammergut, Upper Austria, this is where Klimt photographed the ten exceptional variations of "hanging dresses" worn by Emilie.

Chair intended for Gustav Klimt's studio (Vienna VIII, Josefstädter Straße 21), designed by Josef Hoffmann and made by the Wiener Werkstätte, 1905. Black colored and limed oak. *Gustav Klimt in his blue work smock,* Egon Schiele, circa 1912. Pencil, opaque color, 52.5 x 28 cm. Schiele chose here to represent his elder in his favorite clothes, this indigo blue smock that he wore both for work and his summer leisure pursuits.

Emilie Flöge in a "housecoat". Photo belonging to the series taken by Klimt at Attersee during summer 1906. *Portrait of baroness Elisabeth Bachofen-Echt,* circa 1914. Oil on canvas, 180 x 128 cm. More than a portrait, Klimt often offers an article of "clothing" that places the woman in an almost unreal existence.

Emilie Flöge in an artist's "reform" dress at Attersee. Anonymous photo, circa 1910. By reinterpreting the inelegant fullness of the reform dress in order to meet a need for "natural" freedom, Emilie Flöge and Gustav Klimt reconverted a style long considered inelegant and eccentric into the very latest new thing. *Portrait of Eugenia Primavesi,* 1913-1914. Oil on canvas, 140 x 84 cm. Toyota City Museum, Toyota (Japan).

Shoe design for the Wiener Werkstätte, sketches by Maria Likorz. Pen and water color, circa 1913. The Wiener Werkstätte wanted to highlight the professions of artist and craftsman that are often relegated to second place by industrial production: it became known for this in many areas, including fashion. *Portrait of Madame Primavesi*, circa 1912. Oil on canvas, 150 x 110 cm. The Metropolitan Museum of Art, New York.

"Waldidyl" fabric (forest idyll), Wiener Werkstätte, designed by Carl Otto Czeschka. Sample, 1910-1911. By designing and producing its own fabrics, the Wiener Werkstätte crossed into a new stage. These luxury fabrics, available in a range of many patterns and constantly renewed by the greatest artists of the Werkstätte (Hoffmann, Czeschka and others), allowed Vienna to make a remarkable entry on to the international fashion scene.

Gustav Klimt, host of the Primaveri family – great manufacturers who became the biggest shareholders of the Wiener Werkstätte, financing it until 1925 – participating in an artists' party in the cellar of the Primavesi villa in Winkelsdorf (Moravia), built by Josef Hoffmann. The painter is wearing a suit made out of the Wiener Werkstätte's "Waldidyll" fabric, designed by Carl Otto Czeschka. Circa 1916.

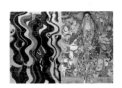

"Marina" fabric, Wiener Werkstätte, designed by Dagobert Peche. Proof on paper, 1911-1912.
Portrait of Friederike Maria Beer, 1916. Oil on canvas, 168 x 130 cm. The Metropolitan Museum of Art, New York. The young woman is wearing an outfit (Turkish style pajama suit) made out of the Wiener Werkstätte's "Marina" fabric, designed by Dagobert Peche.

Portrait of Friederike Maria Beer, Egon Schiele, 1914. Oil on canvas, 190 x 120.5 cm. **"Stichblatt" fabric** (shell), Wiener Werkstätte, designed by Ugo Zovetti. Sample, 1910-1911. **Friederike Maria Beer** wearing a housecoat in the "Stichblatt" fabric. Anonymous photo, circa 1913. Aware of fashion trends and fervent supporter of the Wiener Werkstätte, Friederike Maria Beer is the only woman of this circle to have been painted by both Klimt and Schiele.

Emilie Flöge at Attersee. She is wearing Wiener Werkstätte jewelry that was designed by Kolomon Moser, and an artist's "reform" dress which she probably created in collaboration with Klimt. Autochrome light plaque by Friedrich Walker, circa 1910. *Portrait of woman or Portrait of Ria Munk III*, 1917-1918 (unfinished). Oil on canvas, 180 x 90 cm. Neue Galerie der Stadt, Linz. The ornamentation of portraits by means of the subjects' clothing, make the body itself an ornament.

"Blätter" fabric (leaf), Wiener Werkstätte, designed by Martha Alber, on a BKW (Bruder Kohn Wien) greeting card, 1910-1911.
Portrait of Johanna Staude, 1917/1918 (unfinished). Oil on canvas, 70 x 50 cm. Österreichische Galerie, Vienna. The young woman is also wearing a dress made out of Martha Alber's Wiener Werkstätte "Blätter" fabric.

Emile Flöge in Chinese court clothes, at Attersee. Autochrome light plate by Friedrich Walker, 1913. Emilie Flöge is wearing a Chinese dress here, but she had also assembled an impressive collection of rustic lace and embroidery from Romania and eastern Austria-Hungary. She had begun to incorporate these fragments long before regionalist popular styles came into vogue.

Gustav Klimt and Emilie Flöge in the garden of Klimt's studio, circa 1905-1906. Emilie Flöge is wearing a "reform" dress, probably created by Koloman Moser. Photo: Moriz Nähr. **Portrait of Gustav Klimt,** 1914. He is photographed by his friend Anton Josef Troka (called Antios), who was an amateur photographer before he opened a studio in Vienna. He is known today for his portraits of artists, particularly the portraits of Egon Schiele, of whom he was also a friend.

The author and the publishers thank the Galerie Welz (Salzbourg), the Österreichische Galerie (Vienna) and Wolfgang G. Fischer (Vienna-London) for giving them permission to reproduce the paintings, photos and other documents. They also thank the photographic archives Austrian Archives (Vienna) who provided all of the other illustrations.